Christmas Already!

Gray Jolliffe, father of three and husband of one, has finally given up all hope of being a test pilot. Instead, he has yielded to parental pressure and become a cartoonist.

'Art runs in the family,' he explains 'In fact, Art won the ¼ mile at Yaxley sports back in '63.' Gray had the misfortune to be bombed during the war (in Cornwall) and the resulting brain damage now manifests itself in this sordid collection of profane gags. What he particularly likes about cartooning is the total absence of challenge.

D0785400

Notice anything?

Christmas Already!

Written and illustrated
by Gray Jolliffe

ARROW BOOKS

Arrow Books Limited
17-21 Conway Street, London W1P 6JD

An imprint of the Hutchinson Publishing Group

London Melbourne Sydney Auckland
Johannesburg and agencies throughout
the world

First published by Essex House Publishing 1978
This revised and expanded edition first published
by Arrow Books 1982

© illustrations and text Gray Jolliffe 1978, 1982 ·

This book is sold subject to the condition that it shall not,
by way of trade or otherwise, be lent, resold, hired out, or
otherwise circulated without the publisher's prior consent
in any form of binding or cover other than that in which it
is published and without a similar condition including
this condition being imposed on the subsequent
purchaser.

Set in Baskerville

Made and printed in Great Britain
by The Guernsey Press Co Ltd
Guernsey, Channel Islands

ISBN 0 09 930060 5

Bit of a tricky one, this. We want a Jewish gag-book about Christmas - mildly offensive, but not over the top - light but uncompromising - no filth - a bit naughty, but don't overdo it. Get the picture?
BRIEF

Business is terrible! Somehow, we must find a way of making a little prophet!

Knock up a man's wife? What kind of angel would I be if I agreed to a thing like that??

Take it easy, Romeo! First you have to buy me dinner!

1.

2.

3.

4.

Of course he's gay! Do you think I'm a virgin because I like it?

It was great, babe, but now I gotta fly!

Santa Claus? No bubeleh, I'm Santa Cohen. Wanna buy a present?

Oy – you dropped one of your flip-flops.

*OK – pregnant is only a few lousy months – but this I have to wear
all my life?*

Sing, they don't. Hum, they most certainly do!

And here's another one for the kid when he gets here . . . size one.

*And there's just one other thing, Tracy. God would like you to
change your name to Mary.*

Feathers? You been eating chicken in bed again?

And since then, doctor, how often does he call me? How many flowers do I get? What do I hear about maintenance? You're right — a big fat zero!

How can you afford to give away all these presents?..
I robbed a bank!
I could never do a thing like that!
Too honest, huh?
No - I can't get a stocking over my head!

It should arrive about December 25 – maybe Boxing Day . . .

Different lipstick? New gown? Okay, I give up. What's different?

*So this *is* where you get your red nose!*

I'm pregnant, you old faggot! Figure that one out!

Production is never a problem. It's the distribution that knackers us!

What do you mean, I can't be. I am and you'd better believe it!

A pregnant virgin is weird enough, but that thing over your head that won't go away has us totally foxed!

*It's Christmas, I'm pregnant, God knows how — and now you tell
me you forgot to make a reservation! Terrific!*

Age next birthday?

I'm sorry sir, we just do not have a room. Even for a Gold credit card.

Smith? That's a new one. Most of them put Cohen!

And where's the ladies' powder room . . . ?

Let him try it. He's the one with the nose.

Be reasonable – at least the conception was immaculate!

A digital watch? Are you crazy? What kind of reindeer wears a digital watch?

Because Caesar's Palace is way beyond our means, that's why!

Face it, Claus – you need a totally different size of garment to go round all those latkes!

Uh-oh! It's at Bernie's place. That's a bad start!

Room Service . . . one bucket of boiling water, one bottle of Scotch Whi . . .

All this happening and you can eat?

We better get this show on the road. Who's driving, you or me?

Hurry up?? Listen – next time you *bloody well carry the gold!*

Ask yourself Mr Claus . . . how can I justify a further facility to someone who appears so consistently in the red?

This is positively the last Christmas I'm spending with your family!

JC? That's nice! We're AC/DC.

Tell you what, Sunshine – let's have a couple more and miss out Poland.

This is the part that always breaks me up!

We were praying for a boy, so I guess somewhere there must be a God . . .

A Capricorn yet! I too am a Capricorn! God's children, us Capricorns!

Ah – you found *us okay then?*

Okay, okay, Libya — but I'm telling you — you'll hate *it!*

A lowly stable they said, but this lowly I didn't expect!

C'mon boss — it's gone four and we've still got Africa to do!

So where's the herald angels?

So what did you expect with a one-star hotel?

The gold is his Christmas present. For his birthday, we have this other stuff!

The gold is nice. Frankincense and myrrh we have plenty of!

Am I to understand, then, that you are not a meshuggener who's convinced he's Santa Claus, but Santa Claus who's convinced he's a meshuggener . . .?

And finally – a life subscription to his trade journal.

There's no mistaking who's the father — look at that nose!

And what do I get for Christmas? Zilch, that's what I get.

It's plastic! Nice huh?

Where have you been to get your schmatteh in such a state?

Do you know who that is out there? That's Mr and Mrs Christ, and their little boy, the Messiah! And where do you put them? In the goddam stable, you klutz! Five martinis on the house is how you say sorry!

The wise men say chicken soup at his age isn't wise . . .

Relax Sharon! It's me! Solly Strumpfenberg!

Of course it's home-made. You try buying whisky this time of night in the bible belt!

Tell her I got it wholesale and you'll have more than a red nose!

Of course, the real joke is he's not even the father!

Not tonight, Rabbi. Tomorrow can you come back?

And this is for you Rudie. It ain't much, but it's something I've always wanted!

Every Christmas he gets like this, the bum.

'Not the father?' I said. 'Then who is? An Angel?? You're putting me on!'

One day, son, I want you should do your Momma a favour — work a miracle on your father . . .

Last stop Barbados! Good thinking Rudie!

Already he's started!

So if he's just an ordinary kid, what's this — a bagel?

. . . According to research, Santa Claus is non profit-making!
Ho, Ho, Ho!

Why didn't you say you were having a Messiah? I would have given you the penthouse suite!

Father Who?

It's my first night in the new job – boy, what a schlep!

If you'd been there, you could have had one!

Trade in? With 94303472143091117239009327I miles on the clock? Do me a favour!

Well, suppose I told you I got friends in high places? Would that persuade the goddam bar to open again?

'Bye then . . . Terrific to meet you! Funny to think that only last Christmas you didn't think there was any such thing as God, and I thought Santa Claus was the opiate of the masses . . .

I think he's going to be an intellectual. Who in God's name can he take after?

. . . They even sang one called 'Camel ye Faithful'.

1.

2.

3.

4.

If that's a Messiah, Becky, I'm a camel's poopik . . .